D0577071

ELLE DECOR
PORTFOLIOS

KITCHENS

Cover: photo © Marianne Haas
Reportage Marie-Claire Blanckaert

Translated from French by Simon Pleasance and Fronza Woods
Copyedited by Matthew Malady

ISBN: 2 85018 740 2

Color separation: HAFIBA

Printed in France by Clerc

KITCHENS

filipacchi publishing

Friendliness incarnate, the kitchen is increasingly replacing the dining room and living room as the favorite gathering place in many households.

Needless to say, it must be functional, first and foremost, but people also want their kitchens to be welcoming and attractive. For this, today, all the know-how and resources of professional interior designers and decorators can be called upon.

This little book will take you into the kitchens of luminaries like Calvin Klein and design magnate Terence Conran, but also those of simpler people who have managed to arrange this "crossroads" of the hearth and home with taste and imagination.

You will find every kind of style here, from "country" atmospheres combining old materials, secondhand objects, and an eye on comfort, to more contemporary—or even eccentric—kitchens that play with modern design, furniture with clean, refined lines, and high-tech household appliances.

Storage tips, plus useful manufacturers' addresses, and the finest materials, make this visit to the most beautiful *Elle Decor* kitchens a must for anyone dreaming of creating a kitchen that becomes a genuine living room.

CONTENTS

KITCHENS
DINING ROOMS

FRIENDLINESS INCARNATE, THE KITCHEN IS INCREASINGLY REPLACING THE DINING ROOM. IT HAS TO BE WELCOMING, BUT FUNCTIONAL AT THE SAME TIME. TO MEET THESE EXPECTATIONS, INGENIOUSLY, THE KNOW-HOW AND TALENTS OF INTERIOR DECORATORS AND DESIGNERS ARE CALLED UPON.

Left. In a triplex in Lyons, architect Rémi Tessier played with the lighting by creating a light shaft that serves as the principal light source for the whole kitchen. He paid close attention to the materials and their color—the furnishings are made of wenge and woven wood and the central table is slate. **Above.** In his home near New York City, Calvin Klein elected to respect traditional New England style. The old floor is made of large planks of blackened pine. resembling ebony.

KITCHENS
DINING ROOMS

A new stylistic direction for English interior decorators Anthony Collett and David Champion is evident in this large and erstwhile Victorian apartment in the heart of London. At once welcoming and refined, the kitchen has fitted oak cupboards, which they designed. The cornice, decorated with an array of celadon platters interspersed with sheafs of wheat concealing loudspeakers, is a salient feature of this room. In the foreground, a very handsome arts & crafts table with matching chairs conjures up the spirit of a country kitchen.

10

KITCHENS DINING ROOMS

Top left. Jacques Bon and his wife established the Hotel du Mas de Peint in a Camargue farmstead. Meals are eaten together in the kitchen, where farm produce is the fare as often as possible. The oval table is an old cellarman's table, and the traditional stove is by Morice. The old copper chandelier was unearthed by decorator Estelle Reale-Garcin.
Below left. This traditional kitchen is one of the gathering-places for the residents of a castle in the Tours region of France. It was restored by decorator and antique-dealer Alain Demachy. The predominant color in the kitchen is black, but the room is arranged to make it very lively and bright: terra cotta tiles cover the floor, and the walls are clad with oblong black tiles. The working surfaces are made of vertical wooden slats, that resemble butchers' blocks.
Right. This kitchen, in a London apartment, was redone by Anthony Collett and David Champion.
Notice how the pale hue of the limed oak contrasts with the bold counterpoint of the black granite worktop.
The table and chairs are in the arts & crafts style.

Left and right. Valérie Solvit. the head of a communications agency. and her husband. Antoine. have always dreamed of owning a home in the heart of Paris. Their wish has come true in this duplex apartment. designed with the help of their antique-dealer friend. Christian Sapet. The rooms on the lower floor are the living room. the children's bedrooms. the library. and the kitchen. For Valérie. "luxury is mixing things." So

she contrasted beiges, taupe, and blacks, to which she added touches of red and green. Black predominates in the kitchen and its dining room area, lit by many lamps. The ambience created is intentionally convivial, so that the kitchen would become the area where meals were eaten. The walls are painted matt black and the working surface is made of crazed lava. The kitchen and dining room floors are wooden parquet.

Left. In this home. designed by Philippe Starck. the kitchen is part and parcel of the life of the living room. The well-lit working surface is flanked on each side by shelves of dark-stained wood and white lacquered cupboards with simple chromium-plated handles. The chandelier is in Venetian glass.

Above. Donna Karan's Long Island kitchen is functional and inviting. and often serves as a dining room for quick lunches. The central island. used for preparing food. is transformed into a dining table in such occasions. The white color and the view of nature conspire to create a sense of serenity.

17

KITCHENS
DINING ROOMS

When Andrew Zarzycki and his wife, Jill, set out to redesign their London home in the heart of Chelsea, they were keen to apply a contemporary spirit to classical architectural principles: axes, symmetry, and proportions. Andrew readily admits that he is inspired by Jean-Michel Frank, Adolf Loos, Joseph Pleznick, and Hans Van Der Laan. He designed the maplewood kitchen furnishings which were then made by John Spencer Joinery. The black stone working surface comes from Pietra San Marco. Conceived by the master of the house, the stove and extractor hood were designed by Gaggenau. Zulu baskets made of braided telephone wire embellish the heavy oak table, made by Matthew Collins—a craftsman who is invariably entrusted with the furniture that Andrew designs. The black leather chairs are by Mario Bellini.

KITCHENS
DINING ROOMS

Left. This kitchen using beige and white hues, was designed by decorators Anthony Collett and David Champion. It features cabinets in waxed maple, and the huge copper extractor hood, which soars over the hotplates, catches the eye immediately. The black granite working surface matches the grey slate floor, which is covered by sea-grass matting. The room is a proper dining room with its round, cloth-covered table and its upholstered chairs lending it refined look.

Right. Advertising executive Eric Poisson enlisted the services of decorators Jacques Grange and Christian Benais for the renovation of a castle built on the heights overlooking Nice in the early 20th century. They achieved a happy marriage between ancient and modern in this large kitchen/dining room. The painted ceiling of the former study overlooks a genuine, professional "range." The large copper family chandelier is a 19th century remake of a 17th century Dutch model. The wood and granite table was designed by Eric Poisson.

KITCHENS
DINING ROOMS

When the three giants of British interior design—Anthony Collett, David Champion, and John MacLeod—arrived in Switzerland on the shores of Lake Constance to renovate this castle, the first thing they did was open up the interior spaces to the natural light and outstanding view. The kitchen illustrates the success of this idea. It is bathed in light and overlooks a garden inspired by Monet's at Giverny. Cherry wood is used throughout, and the working surfaces are in black granite. A huge table—with its oak top sanded and bleached—stands in the middle of the room. The blinds are electrically controlled, and the nearby beams serve as supports for wrought iron lights designed by Collett and Champion.

22

CONTEMPORARY
KITCHENS

FOR THOSE DRAWN TO CONTEMPORARY STYLE, THE KITCHEN OFFERS A CHANCE TO PLAY WITH MATERIALS, FURNITURE, AND HIGH-TECH APPLIANCES. AND EVERYONE CAN EXPRESS THEMSELVES ACCORDING TO THEIR NEEDS—WITH SPARE, SOPHISTICATED, AND ALWAYS FUNCTIONAL LINES.

Left. Interior designer Christian Liaigre's kitchen—on the Ile de Ré, on France's Atlantic coast—combines simplicity and elegance. The large, working surface made of oiled teak, with its blackened doors, accommodates a Czech & Speake sink and stainless steel hotplates. Teak shelving is used for storing utensils and dishes.

Above. In this kitchen, organized around a central island, the cherry wood doors were designed by Pepe Tanzi for Boffi. The ovens and the grill are by Gaggenau, the extractor hood in stainless steel and glass is by Atag, and the refrigerator is by General Electric. The floor is covered with natural flagstones.

Left. Designed by interior designer Rémi Tessier in Lyons, this kitchen is in pale and dark sycamore with a Cenia stone worktop. The kitchen connects with the other rooms like in a loft, which means that the light circulates throughout.
Above left. In Brussels, Axel Verhoustraeten created this kitchen entirely with fired fiberboard and stainless steel.

The stainless steel table has matching utensils and the floor is in Cascaie marble.
Above right. Redesigned by Agnès Comar, this Valais chalet combines Swiss tradition and modern comfort. The kitchen furniture and floor are in natural birch, while the working surface is slate. The extractor hood and oven are by Gaggenau.

CONTEMPORARY KITCHENS

In this Corsican home,
where the interior space
opens generously onto the world
outside, large windows survey
the majestic seascape.
As a result, the kitchen
dining room, and living room
are all awash in light.
The idea for the stainless
steel cupboard doors came
from a bar at Fizaris airport.
The working surface is made
of Corsican granite.

CONTEMPORARY KITCHENS

Above. Same kitchen as the one described on pages 28-29.
Right. From the dining room in this house in the heart of Brussels, we see a kitchen dominated by light shades of color. In designing this space, architect Jean-Laurent Périer drew upon Californian, Nordic, and Colonial influences. The structure, along with the doors and kitchen cupboards, are painted in the same blue-grey distemper. The counter tops are made of white corian, and the walls are covered with large, matt white tiles.

30

Left. Interior decorator François Catroux makes his home in a Parisian apartment. where he has managed to create an extremely austere but warm ambience. In keeping with the other rooms. the kitchen is done in white. beige and brown tones which help to set off the Persian blinds on all the windows. This room. which doubles as a dining room. is in oak. A generous wine rack is suspended in the wall above the table.

Above. Interior decorator Marc Held's kitchen. in Paris. reflects his fondness for detail. The kitchen unit. configured like a bar. is covered with marine plywood. and one side can be folded down to make more room. A delightful atmosphere emanates from this nook beneath the sloping roof. where every effort has been made to use the space without taking away from the comfort of the room.

CONTEMPORARY KITCHENS

Above. Suspended between sky and water. magnate of English design Terence Conran makes his home in the upper reaches of a building surveying the Thames in London. The kitchen has been designed as a professional space—marble work counter in the center. chopping block—and a strong sense of real kitchen and pantry. The stools and long oak table. doubling as a sideboard. were originally designed for a restaurant. Light plays a major role in this room. located on the same floor as the dining room and living room. Light pours through the glass roof and long windows. sculpting the volume by highlighting the wooden banister and rough concrete columns.

Above. In the heart of a village on the Vendée coast, perfume creator Annick Goutal and her husband have made their dream come true. The couple has created a home where they can enjoy quiet hours of work and relaxation, and leave all that Parisian stress far behind them. The result of their hard work is a well-lit and welcoming home, where the decoration has evolved in tune with favorite whims and wishes. All the rooms are arranged around a sunny courtyard, into which the kitchen opens. As in the case with every room on the ground floor, the kitchen is painted white.

Above. The arrangement of this kitchen, organized along symmetrical axes and around a central island, has retained classical touches in a contemporary spirit. The pure lines of the furniture, seats, and appliances mix perfectly with old-style cornices and a brick ceiling. The kitchen was designed by Grégoire Bignier and made by Bulthaup. The floor is oak, while the cupboards are made of beech wood.

Right. Decorator Oddes has applied his amazing knowledge of materials to the design of his Parisian loft. The kitchen walls were covered in plaster, clay, and sienna before being waxed, so that the daylight would bring out the colors to their fullest. One counter is made of medium density fiberboard (MDF) and stainless steel, another of MDF and beech. The extractor hood—along with the round sink, was made by Francke—is supported by a stainless steel pier. The cooking plates are by Gaggenau.

Above. By removing the interior walls in a small 17th century building near the Bastille in Paris, interior decorator Nicole Lehmann has breathed new life back into this town house. As the kitchen well illustrates, one of her priorities was to bring light into every room, regardless of its connection to natural light sources. One way of doing this was to create floors made of glass tiles. Following the 1930s' style chosen throughout the house, the kitchen has a very striking personality. It was made by the Serre Company, using carefully designed colors and materials. The chairs are by Mallet-Stevens. The frieze of irregular tiles on the floor echoes the room's basic hues: green for the glass, grey for the stainless steel, and beige for the stone-like rendering.

Above. In southernmost Corsica, an Americomania fell in love with a plot of land overlooking the sea at Sperone. He then entrusted Guy Breton with the task of creating a Californian house on the property. The owner wanted to be able to gaze at the sea from every room, including the kitchen.

The decoration here combines wood and aluminum in most unexpected ways. Aluminum bistro doors seal off the storage cupboards.

Around the pine table, a set of American chairs —the "Institutional Chair"— in light aluminum. derive from The Conran Shop. Porthole lights add an original touch to the decoration.

Above and right. Near the Ourcq canal in Paris, architect Hervé Vermesch has converted an old tannery into a superb home. He did so by respecting the building's industrial structure. The fluidity and voluminous effect of an industrial loft have thus been preserved. No room has been completely walled off, and pillars have been used to separate different areas of the home.

Above. The kitchen is fitted with a soap stone working surface and a cathedral glass extractor hood. Large damask stone tiles are affixed to the walls.

Right. Here we have a view of the entrance to the kitchen. On the floor, the parquet has been painted in two shades of grey to give the illusion of a carpet. The bar is in the foreground.

Above. Because he works in a Manhattan skyscraper, the French journalist living in this Greenwich Village apartment was keen to create a homey atmosphere around him. His kitchen, where he chose to keep an open brick wall at one end, illustrates his success in meeting that goal. On the left, a window is flanked at both ends by cupboards, forming an alcove, where he keeps glasses and dishes. Beneath the window, a small metal display cabinet houses a variety of different objects. The table is by Jeffry Holder, and goes wonderfully with the shades of the wall.

Above. Given the task of restoring a house overlooking Lake Geneva, architect Rémi Tessier decided to combine luxury and rigor. In each room, he has used precious wood. He also designed large windows to usher plenty of light into the heart of the house and make the most of the wonderful view of the lake. His source of inspiration for the kitchen was the Shaker style. He designed every aspect of the room using wild cherry wood. It is sober, functional, and open to the rest of the house. The storage units are methodical and include lots of drawers. But the rigor does not rule out a sense of real comfort.

CONTEMPORARY KITCHENS

Left. In their home in Paris, Bernard Roux and his wife have seen to even the smallest details. The area earmarked for the kitchen includes a central unit covered with Polyrey celadon green laminate, which divides the room into two. The working surface is covered with wenge to create a sense of harmony with the floor. On the left it houses a large stainless steel sink. On the right, tall stools have been brought over from the United States.

Right. Dominique Babigeon's task was to redesign a 19th century town house in Nancy. In doing so, she organized this kitchen so that it became a huge room for living in and replacing the dining room, as the owners requested. Light pours into what was previously a terrace, and the decorations used are quite sober: the kitchen units are in exotic wood, as is the working surface. The floor is oiled oak parquet. The stove and the extractor hood are by Atag. An original idea here is the galvanized steel unit placed to the left of the stove and used for storing kitchen utensils.

CONTEMPORARY KITCHENS

François-Joseph Graf's goal was to thoroughly rethink a vast Parisian apartment. So he transformed a bevy of small dark rooms into an airy, brightly-lit space, that is both classical and contemporary. He gave new lines to the 3,800 sq.ft. home, and created an interplay of perspectives from each one of the rooms. The kitchen, as the hub of the house, illustrates this perfectly. Far from trying to disguise it, François-Joseph Graf has incorporated it into the apartment—using windows that connect the kitchen to the corridor and the same pale oak parquet, so as not to break the unity. Once he finished the design, he entrusted the work to Bulthaup. In the foreground, a La Cornue stove takes center stage. The kitchen furnishings are in grey laminate.

COUNTRY KITCHENS

SINCE THE FUNCTIONAL IS NO LONGER DE RIGUEUR, KITCHENS ARE GETTING BACK THEIR FORMER WARMTH AND COZINESS. THEY CALL TO MIND HOW MUCH WE LOVED THOSE LARGE LIVING ROOMS WITH THEIR LOVELY AROMA OF WAX, AND THE SMELL OF LOGS CRACKLING IN THE HEARTH.

Left. In the Ile-de-France mill where the Fourets live, the kitchen was designed with the help of interior decorator Alain Raynaud. The cupboards are made of sheet metal painted black. The floor is covered with recycled tiles, and the working surface is done in blue and white tiling.

Above. In this Périgord house, a stove has been fitted into an alcove and painted matt black, thus giving the impression of an old-style oven. Above it, a thick slab of slate, cut to size and polished, houses a hotplate.

49

Above. In the home of Parisian decorator Frédéric Méchiche, the functional character of the kitchen does not get in the way of the old-style atmosphere. All the furnishings are in 19th century pine. The warmth of the wood, and the 18th century terra cotta floor, contrasts with the black walls and the grey of the zinc and marble.

Right. This Bulthaup kitchen combines modern materials like beech wood, cracked tiling, and steel, with the charm of old objects. The room is extended by a verandah that adds both light and space.

Left. In Paris, interior decorator Michèle Joubert has created a world where the past is conjured up without any nostalgia. The pantry units are by Henri Quinta. In the center of the room, the

butcher's block in grey stone acts as a working surface. **Above.** In her Atlantic home on the Ile de Ré. Geneviève Lethu has created a semi-professional kitchen where everything is within reach: it is here that her family has its meals. The floor is covered with mottled green granite slabs. which are easy to clean. Walls and storage cupboards are made of shuttering painted matt white. At the far end. beside the American refrigerator. the working surface and wall covering are in stainless steel. The top of the large table is made of Charentes stone. It is surrounded by reproduction Thonet chairs.

Above. This amazing kitchen is right at home in the Paris apartment of designer Christian Astuguevieille. This renowned artist tells a tale through his furniture, and with objects rooted in a highly personal, dreamlike world. His large kitchen also functions as a dining room. The two tables, with their hemp-clad legs and chestnut tops, can be put together or used separately as table and sideboard. The sober, functional sink area has been covered with tiles. The tap fixture is a reproduction of an antique model. On the floor, the old tiling has been kept, and blends nicely with the colors chosen for the room.

Above. In the home that Susie Tompkins-Buell—co-founder of the Esprit brand of clothing—had built in northern California, the kitchen gives an impression of spaciousness that you find throughout the rest of the house. It has a warm feel to it, and is the real soul of the house, leading straight into the dining room. It is made for cooking in, and the tall stools at the central island are designed for quick meals. The factory lights illuminate the working surfaces, and the dishes on the shelves are within easy reach. From the ceiling hangs a mobile of driftwood that was found on the beach.

COUNTRY KITCHENS

Great Belgian chef Roger
Souveyrens and his wife,
renowned decorator Walda
Pairon, designed their home
together. As an antique dealer
in his spare time, Roger is
interested in everything to do
with the table, and the food
placed upon it. In his kitchen,
the table strikes an all-white
note, creating a festive
atmosphere with a subtle
mixture of crystal and
silver-plated objects sharing
the same table with everyday
utensils. In the foreground,
a reproduction Lutyens bench
seat, painted white, blends well
with the painted beams.

Left. Not far from Paris, architect Christian Duval and his wife have converted an old farmhouse into a lovely home. The varnished fir kitchen is the house's gathering place: the hanging baskets give it a homey feeling and the large windows open onto a small courtyard garden perfect for summer days. In the center, a preparation counter with a built-in sink and storage cupboards.

Above. This London kitchen was designed by interior decorator Anthony Collett and made by John Spencer. It is done in oak, and the working surface is in black marble. The floor consists of waxed elm planking. The central table is in oak, and was designed by Anthony Collett. The early 20th century lamp on the far table, and the chair in the foreground, come from Paul Reeves in London. The cast-iron stove on the left is a La Cornue.

Above. In this large residence
in Genoa, the walls of the
high-ceilinged kitchen are
covered with prints, family
photos, paintings, and drawings.
This kitchen-cum-gallery is as
functional as it is hospitable.
A range hood extracts
unpleasant smells, the
appliances are all ultra-modern,
and the waxed parquet adds
to the warm effect of this
friendly kitchen.

Right. The spirit of Provence
holds sway in this very ancient
farmhouse in the Alpilles, north
of the Camargue. It has been
renovated after spending four
decades unhabited. The home's
foundations date back to the
13th century, which explains the
vaults in the oldest part of the
house, where the kitchen is.
Here, the table is laid facing the
large stone fireplace, creating
a scene from bygone days.

60

COUNTRY KITCHENS

Architect Axel Verhoustraeten designed this warm and serviceable kitchen for a house located in a residential neighborhood in Brussels. He opted for slightly greyish, pale sycamore for the furnishings. Ceramic platters rest atop the Classique table, designed by Axel. As in the other rooms, we find furniture by Christian Liaigre—here, stall chairs in sycamore with seats covered in cotton. The working surface is made of oiled blue stone.

63

Above. In the old hunting lodge he lives in on the outskirts of Brussels, couturier Edouard Vermeulen has managed to combine modern design and traditional materials. All the furnishings and household appliances have been covered with broad planks of aged oak. A workshop table stands boldly in the middle of the room. The working surface is in black stone and the chrome-plated nickel taps are by Clek.

Above. In her Paris home, florist Dani decided to install an American-style kitchen bar. The walls of her studio are made of recycled planks. Behind the bar, covered with a sheet of zinc, are the sink,

appliances, hotplates, and oven. The cupboard doors are old shutters. And, while this American-style kitchen concept may be very modern, the atmosphere created in the room is quite rustic at the same time.

Above. In this Provençal farmhouse decorated by Estelle Garcin, the owners have opted for a simple but refined style. Rustic chairs surround a farmhouse table beneath metal lamps. The cast-iron stove is made by Ambassade Renaissance.

Right. In his house in Normandy, actor Pierre Arditi has designed a kitchen where references to the past go hand-in-hand with modern technology. In this former cellar, the floor has been redone in stone and cabochons. Above the working surface is beautiful 18th century tiling from the Farnèse gallery. A Directoire table has center stage. Above the range hood and the oven is a 17th century still life piece depicting a game bag. This central work is surrounded by oil paintings by Pierre's father, Georges Arditi.

Above. In the heart of a new house—but one whose spirit contains all the good qualities that the Flemish tradition has to offer—the kitchen is equipped with professional appliances. Above the La Cornue stove hangs a whole set of stainless steel pans. The surface of the central island, in enameled lava.

partly hides a chopping block. **Above.** Interior decorator Kees van der Valk has done up the Seven One Seven hotel in a 19th century Amsterdam house.

A keen cook, he wanted the kitchen to be spacious and welcoming. A French stove and secondhand bowls surround a working surface made of marble.

COUNTRY KITCHENS

Lampshade designer Marie-Jo Maze-Censier walks down a flight of steps in order to get to the kitchen of her beautiful Paris home. The basement-level kitchen is both large and convivial, and the grand table often serves as a gathering place for friends invited over for dinner. The table is set with great care and is beautifully lit by her own creations.

ECCENTRIC KITCHENS

THE KITCHEN MAY OFTEN BE THE HEART OF THE HOME, BUT IT CAN ALSO BE WHERE ECCENTRICITY IS LET LOOSE. IT MAY ACCOMMODATE THE MOST EXTRAORDINARY CHANDELIERS, OR RECYCLED FURNITURE ALTERED TO SUIT INDIVIDUAL WHIMS. COLORS EXPLODE AND DESIGN HAS FREE REIN.

Left. For a Parisian duplex, decorator Frédéric Méchiche came up with this functional kitchen. The floor is a checkerboard of old marble mosaics. The ceiling has been painted black and the cornice white, so as to match the black and white stripes hand-painted on the end wall. The working surface is in steel, and the furnishings in wild cherry wood. **Above.** In this functional kitchen and dining nook, the kitchen units are in matt beige Formica, while the working surface and buffet are in mottled granite. In the foreground, the sofa is covered with black linen, and the stools are in steel and leather.

ECCENTRIC KITCHENS

Left. This all stainless steel kitchen was built by Bulthaup in an industrial loft in Bruges, Belgium, that was redesigned by the architect Linda Arschoot and her husband Sweet Love. The space is completely open to the outside, and the original structure of this abandoned factory has been preserved. Small metal beams, cupboard doors, and porthole lights are done in the same metal. The floor of the mezzanine, which partly accommodates the kitchen, is made of yellow stoneware.

Right. In the Milan home of decorator Vanna Bellazzi, the kitchen is the pre-eminent room for living in. The walls are covered with plates, dishes, small mirrors, and other unique items picked up on bargain hunts. The 19th century table comes from a printing works. The Viennese chairs date from the Secession (Montessi and Garau in Milan). The striking chandelier is a combination of iron and pendant stones.

In a classic farmhouse in the Alpilles, just north of Arles, Maxime de La Falaise has created a Baroque home for her friend Sarah Saint-George. The daring and eye-catching design suits Saint-George perfectly.

Right. Above the green Aga stove, the Godin hood has swapped its copper for the simplicity of stainless steel. In the foreground, a long butcher's block that was unearthed in the Béarn, in the western Pyrenees, reveals a secret drawer. On the left, a cupboard painted by Maxime and an Andy Warhol canvas.

Above. The wicker drawers in this Aga stove unit hold cutlery and table linen. The marble sink and the taps are quite old. The mosaic is a mixture of gravel, pebbles, and bits of Venetian glass.

ECCENTRIC KITCHENS

Above. The kitchen of architects Jean-Louis and Mado Mellerio is the only brightly colored room in their apartment. The atmosphere is convivial, with a central stove and island, which also serves as a table for informal meals with friends. The room was made by Bulthaup and the kitchen appliances are by Gaggenau. **Right.** When adman Bruno Le Moult asked Phlippe Starck to design his home in the Ile Saint-Germain in Paris, the result was an impressive space of concrete, glass, marble, and aluminum, for light to play off of. The kitchen is spectacular. The sink, in a block of marble, matches a floor covered in the same material. Against the far wall, there is room for a stainless steel worktop, a hotplate, and cupboards in sandblasted glass.

78

ECCENTRIC KITCHENS

In her Parisian loft, the grande dame of decoration and design, Andrée Putman, offers a grandiose demonstration of her talent. She likes confronting the modest with the precious, and the modern with the not so modern. The kitchen opens onto the terrace. By day, light comes in through the huge glass roof and wall, and by night it is lit by simple farmhouse lights adjusted by counterweights. Here, everything is visible and within easy reach. On the walls are works by Niki de Saint-Phalle and Bram van Velde. Below, the chairs are by Kohn, and, to the left of the door leading outside a Thonet armchair. On the table, two 1900 plant-motif candlesticks.

80

STORAGE
TIPS

ACHIEVING ORDERLINESS IS NO MEAN FEAT, AND FOR TIDINESS FREAKS, SHELVES, CUPBOARDS, AND DRAWERS ARE NEVER BEAUTIFUL AND EFFICIENT ENOUGH. BUT WHEN IT COMES TO THE QUALITY OF THEIR MANUFACTURE, THEY CAN BE WONDERFULLY INCORPORATED IN THE KITCHEN.

Left. This lacquered white unit was designed by Popy Moreni for storing dishes, kitchenware and groceries. With its variety of compartments, this unit can hold bottles of wine and dishes, ceramic pots and cutlery.

Above. Fashion designer Agnès Comar created this interior fitting for a yacht and found clever ways of storing things in small spaces. The compartments for dishes were designed so that nothing is broken in heavy seas.

83

STORAGE TIPS

This handy item designed by Toncelli will delight the obsessive: a glass-covered drawer where each utensil has its slot on a mahogany background. The pear wood nutcracker and utensils are by Twergy.

Left. Rena Dumas' services were enlisted to design the interior of a major French industrialist's private aircraft, so she instantly invented the most sophisticated and luxurious of storage units. Each piece and dish has its very own leather-lined slot. Teapots, jugs, and sugar-bowls are by Mariage Frères.

Above right. Monique Duveau salvaged this pretty piece of furniture. It is likely that this item was formerly used by a seed merchant. In it, she has methodically arranged her food stocks, and each drawer is carefully labeled. The solid lower drawers are used for her small gardening tools.

Right. These cleverly designed Bulthaup storage units can also be slipped in between shelves. The wooden containers are available in several sizes and come with handles. The terra cotta dish keeps bread fresh. Its solid wooden lid also serves as a bread board.

STORAGE TIPS

Far left. Architect Rémi Tessier designed some of the kitchen furniture in a beautiful triplex in Lyons. This glass-fronted storage cabinet is made of wenge and woven wood, and offers a glimpse of some Muriel Grateau glassware.

Left. In Patricia and Philippe Hurel's home, the kitchen cupboards are made of bleached ash, and separate the kitchen from the dining room. In the lower unit, which boasts an ingenious false back system, dishes and glassware are on display on the dining room side, while pots and pans and other practical utensils are visible on the kitchen side.

STORAGE TIPS

Left. This countertop features a luxurious marble and mahogany storage unit. The large stainless steel bins are used for storing beans and spices, which are visible through the glass front. The blender is from KitchenAid; the cheese board and wire stand come from The Conran Shop.

Right. These long and heavy wooden spice drawers contain removable stainless steel storage drawers. The cast iron scales are by La Cornue.

STORAGE TIPS

Left. In Pierre Bergé's home at Saint-Rémy-de-Provence, a kitchen wall has been designed to hold bottles of wine. This rack, made of painted pine wood, is for wines that are drunk every day, and saves one trip down to the cellar. Beneath the worktop counter, Bergé has arranged baskets for storing cutlery and small kitchen utensils.

Right. In Monique Duveau's home, shelving units by Metro System fit nicely into a kitchen corner. It is extremely functional, and the height of the shelves can be altered as required.

STOVES

KITCHEN ENTHUSIASTS LOVE THESE PERENNIALLY FASHIONABLE ANTIQUE MODELS, MODERNIZED JUST ENOUGH TO MAKE THEM TRULY PROFESSIONAL. BENEATH THEIR YESTERYEAR CHARM, THEY HIDE A KNOW-HOW BASED ON SOUND TECHNOLOGY.

Left. This timeless stove, individually made since 1900, is the Rolls-Royce of the genre. The front is in vitrified enamel, and the frame in nickel-plated steel and bronze. It is a combined electric and gas stove, and it has two ovens, a grill, and a deep fryer. This is the La Cornue Le Château model. Width 58 in. depth 25 in. **Above.** The impressive Retour d'Egypte stove, in the home of Christine and Michel Guérard, was designed by Christine and made by Molteni.

95

STOVES

Bottom left. This is a traditional Cluny stove in enameled stainless steel with five gas burners, two ovens, and vitrified, polished anti-acid enamel interior.
Lacanche. 39 x 24 x 32 in.

Top left. This C519 stove, with five gas burners and a multi-purpose electric Gastronome oven, performs self-cleaning by catalysis.
SMEG. 35 x 23 x 34 in.

Top right. This rustic Rosane stove in enameled steel and brass, features four burners (three gas and one electric hotplate), and natural convection by catalysis.
Rosières. 23 x 23 x 34 in.

Center right. Here we have a Souveraine stove with a gas oven, drawers for pots and pans, a storage cabinet, and cook top with five gas burners.
Godin. 43 x 22 x 34 in.

Bottom right. This Petite Maman stove in enameled stainless steel features chrome-plated finish, a stainless steel surface with three gas burners, and an electric oven.
La Cornue. 28 x 23 x 37 in.

96

STOVES

Left page.
Left. This C246 FGEA Tradition stove is fitted with a self-cleaning oven. It is enameled and contains a burn-proof cold door, seven cooking functions, an electric hotplate and three gas burners. Scholtès. 23 x 23 x 34 in.
Right. The Big Size stove is made of curved glass, stainless steel and corian. Its integrated induction top has four burners. It has a multi-purpose oven and a traditional oven, as well as two storage drawers. DeDietrich. 23 x 30 x 37 in.

Right page.
Above. This gas stove with four burners has a self-cleaning catalytic oven and a wide door made of tinted mirror glass. Faure. 23 x 23 x 32 in.
Below. Here is a professional stove for private homes, in chrome-plated stainless steel. The top is in cast iron with two burners hotplate. It has a large gas oven. 55 x 31 x 33 in. This Itaque model was designed by Alain Ducasse for Molteni.

Above. This La Châtelaine stove comes from a line of stoves that first appeared back in 1842. It features satin-finished steel and brass, and has a self-cleaning oven with rotisserie, grill, four electronically lit gas burners, and a reversible grill plate. Godin. 43 in long and 27 in deep.

Right. This Aga stove with an enameled front, cooks with gas. Of English manufacture, it was designed in 1929 by Gustav Dalen, winner of the Nobel prize for physics. It stores heat in accumulators, and features two hotplates, a roasting oven, and a copper steaming oven. It can also provide hot water.

FURNITURE

TWO-TIER STORAGE UNITS, TABLES WITH SHELVES, LINEN CUPBOARDS, THESE KITCHEN UNITS ONLY HAVE PLUS POINTS. WE LOVE THEM BECAUSE THEY ARE CONVENIENT, ADJUSTABLE, COMPACT, AND EVEN NOMADIC.

Above. This heavy alder work table is fitted with large drawers made of varnished wicker and a tin surface. Grange.
W 62 in x d 31 in x h 35 in.
Left page.
Back. Strictly for gourmets, this two-tier piece is in wild cherry wood. In the top half, one can keep bottles of wine and kitchen aids. The doors of the lower sideboard unit are covered with fine wire mesh, ideal for storing cheeses! La Cornue.
W 47 in x d 26 in x h 81 in.
Front. This 1930s' style bistro linen cupboard is in wild cherry wood, with its top in brass-edged tin. Roche-Bobois.
W 44 in x d 31 in x h 35 in.

Above. This aluminum unit, with drawers and a shelf, accommodates a System 20 washing-up unit, with basin compartment in the center, a draining basket, faucets and counter.

The 12 in. glass splashboard and paper towel dispenser is optional. Bulthaup. W 51 in x d 28 in x 37 in. **Right.** This "130" unit in steel and aluminum is called "Standing." It was designed

by Lino Codato. This model is fitted with an oven unit, hood, working surface, shelf, cupboard and drawers in stainless steel. Roche-Bobois. W 51 in x d 26 in x 83 in.

FURNITURE

This Dauphine oak unit has
a very natural feel about it.
The working surface is in
treated beech wood, the sink
is earthenware, and the faucets
are in chrome-plated copper
and faience.
Flamant.
W 85 in x d 27 in x h 40 in.

FURNITURE

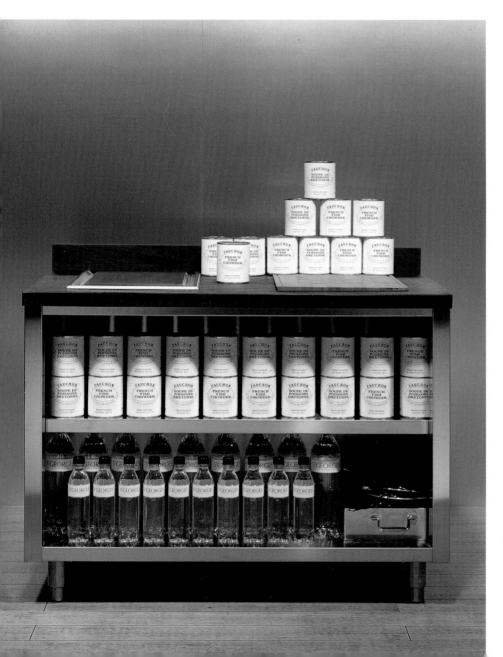

Left. This shelved table is in stainless steel. The working surface is slate. It is fitted with a Teppen Yaki Japanese grill by Atag and a removable wooden chopping board that is easy to clean. The unit can also be fitted with a sink and other cooking appliances. Shore.
W 47 in x d 26 in x h 35 in.

Right. This Varde unit is made of particle board with white birch veneer. The worktop contains a stainless steel sink. It also includes a Eloquence oven and a stainless steel Scholtès hotplate. Ikea.
W 57 in x d 25 in x h 35 in.

1

2

ACCESSORIES

FROM THE WHISTLING JAPANESE KETTLE TO THE POTATO MASHER BY WAY OF THE VEGETABLE PEELER AND THE NUTCRACKER, ALL THESE MINOR KITCHEN ACCESSORIES AND UTENSILS ARE AT ONCE CHARMING AND PRACTICAL, BRIGHT, AND NICE TO LOOK AT.

1. April oyster knife with plastic handle.
2. Adjustable lobster cracker, designed not to break the meat.
3. Multi-purpose kitchen scissors.

4. For opening the lids on glass jars, this instrument has a steel blade that can be lengthened and shortened.
5. Anna Pepper pepper grinder by A. Mendini for Alessi.

ACCESSORIES

6

7

8

9

10

16

17

18

19

11

12

13

14

15

21

20

12. Brushed aluminum pasta tongs.
13. Rösle flat whisks. No lumps guaranteed!
14. Butter curl, bottle opener, slicer and milk can piercer, all-in-one, in steel.
15. Graphic but practical Rösle sauce spoons.
16. Light, whistling Japanese kettle in matt steel.
17. Steel meat-ball tongs.
18. Asparagus peeler in stainless steel.
19. Ideal basket-like shelter for boiling eggs.
20. An articulated steamer basket that fits in a casserole or pan, diameter from 6 to 9 in.
21. Squirrel nutcracker in stainless steel.

6. Chily Penguin refrigerator thermometer, in steel by Oscar Tusquets for Alessi.
7. This very easy to handle nutcracker can open any kind of nut with its Crackerjack ratchet system.
8. Old-style stainless steel wire spoon and ladle. Ikea.
9. Rösle potato masher in stainless steel.
10. Fishbone tongs in stainless steel.
11. Rotary egg-beater (for purists).

ACCESSORIES

22

23

24

25

26

27

28

29

30

31

Sowden Design for Alessi.
24. Diabolix bottle opener in plastic by Biagio Cisotti for Alessi.
25. Easy to use corkscrew with levers.
26. Fine sieve.
27. Citrus zester and knife.
28. Reloadable gas lighter using a cigarette lighter (with safety catch for children).
29. Dual-purpose kitchen scissors doubling as bottle opener.
30. Vegetable peeler.
31. Spiral vegetable cutter for shaping fruit and vegetables, Thai-style.

22. Classic but cool Bialetti Neapolitan espresso coffee machine: it comes in green, yellow, and black.
23. Plastic Alphonse timer.

ACCESSORIES

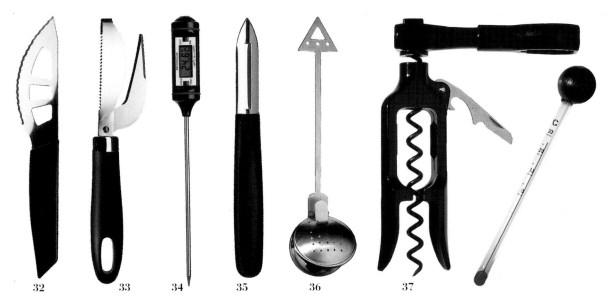

32   33   34   35   36   37

38

32. Rubber-handled pizza knife.
33. Japanese fish knife with
scale remover.
34. Electric kitchen
thermometer.
35. Single blade, right-handed
peeler designed so that
peelings don't get caught in it.
36. One-cup tea infuser.
37. Pocket corkscrew (it can
be taken apart) sold with a
thermometer and capsule cutter
in a wooden box. Screwpull.

39   40   41   42   43   44

45

38. Ultra-chic scales in cast iron and chrome with weights. Galerie La Cornue.
39, 40, 41. Skimmer, spatula and salad server in stainless steel, designed by Philippe Starck for Alessi.
42, 43. Matt plastic draining spoon and square spatula (for non-stick pans).
44. Mini all-purpose mincer.
45. Garlic storer and press.

117

TILES AND TILING

TILES ARE STILL THE IDEAL BACKDROP FOR ANY ROOM WHERE THE HOME'S HEART BEATS. WHETHER USED AS A SURFACE FOR THE KITCHEN FLOOR OR AS A CLEVER WALL DECO- RATION, TILE IS PRACTICAL, EASY TO CLEAN, TOUGH, AND MORE AND MORE ATTRACTIVE.

Above. In this kitchen, designed by Frédéric Méchiche, a black and white checkerboard effect defies perspective and gives an impression of spaciousness.

Left.
1, 2, 3, 11. Enameled stoneware.
4. Solid enamel.

5. Reproduction stars on enameled terra cotta.
6. Traditional faience.
7. Enameled terra cotta.
8. Enduro tile for heavy use.
9. Enameled industrial terra cotta.
10. Industrial hand-enameled terra cotta.
12. Enameled lava.

Above. Here, with every house she lives in, Loulou de la Falaise projects her personality, her joy in life and exuberance into the decoration and interior design. This kitchen in her home in Normandy is covered with two-colored tiles.

Right. In this kitchen, tiling on the units and furniture is continued on the walls, and the cupboard doors have been limed in the same color as the tiles. The working surface is in enameled lava.

Useful Addresses

GENERAL EQUIPMENT FOR KITCHENS

AGA
(STOVES)
www.aga-rayburn.com
P: 800-633-9200

AMANA (MAYTAG)
(APPLIANCES)
www.amana.com
P: 800-843-0304

ARCLINEA KITCHEN COLLECTION
(KITCHEN DESIGN)
www.arclinea.it
P: 212-758-8370

BOFFI
(CABINETRY)
www.boffi.com
P: 212-431-8282 OR
P: 312-664-9582

BOSCH
(APPLIANCES)
www.boschappliances.com
P: 800-866-2022
(major appliances hotline)
P: 800-944-2904
(home appliances hotline)

BROAN
(APPLIANCES)
www.broan.com
P: 800-558-1711

BSH THERMADOR
(APPLIANCES)
www.thermador.com
P: 800-735-4328

BULTHAUP
(KITCHEN DESIGN)
www.bulthaup.com
P: 800-808-2923

CANAC
(CABINETRY)
www.canackitchens.com
P: 800-226-2248

DACOR
(APPLIANCES)
www.dacor.com
P: 800-793-0093

DOWNSVIEW
(CABINETRY)
www.downsviewkitchens.com
P: 905-677-9354

DYNAMIC COOKING SYSTEMS
(APPLIANCES)
www.dcsappliances.com
P: 800-433-8466

ELKAY ELITE GOURMET SINKS
(PLUMBING)
www.elkay.com
P: 630-574-8484

FISHER & PAYKEL
(APPLIANCES)
www.fisherpaykel.com
P: 800-863-5394

GAGGENAU
(BUILT-IN APPLIANCES)
www.gaggenau.com/us
P: 800-828-9165

GENERAL ELECTRIC
(APPLIANCES)
www.ge.com
P: 800-626-2000

GREAT INDOORS
(APPLIANCES)
www.thegreatindoors.com
P: 847-286-2500

KENMORE
(APPLIANCES)
www.kenmore.com
P: 888-KENMORE

KOHLER & KALLISTA
(PLUMBING, DESIGN)
www.kohler.com
P: 800-4-KOHLER
www.kallista.com
P: 888-4-KALLISTA

KWC FAUCETS
(PLUMBING)
www.kwcfaucets.com
P: 800-KWCFCTS

LACANCHE
(STOVES)
www.lacancheusa.com
P: 800-570-CHEF

LA CORNUE
(STOVES)
www.purcellmurray.com
P: 800-892-4040

MERILLAT
(CABINETRY)
www.merillat.com
P: 866-850-8557

MIELE
(APPLIANCES)
www.mieleusa.com
P: 800-843-7231

PLAIN & FANCY
(CABINETRY)
www.plainfancycabinetry.com
P: 800-447-9006

POGGENPOHL
(KITCHEN DESIGN)
www.poggenpohlusa.com
P: 800-987-0553

POLIFORM/VARENNA
(KITCHEN DESIGN)
www.varenna.com
P: 877-VARENNA

RUTT
(KITCHEN DESIGN,
CABINETRY)
www.rutt1.com
P: 800-220-7888

SIEMATIC
(KITCHEN DESIGN)
www.siematic.com
P: 800-959-0109

SNAIDERO
(KITCHEN DESIGN)
www.snaidero.com
P: 310-516-8499

SUB-ZERO/WOLF
(APPLIANCES)
www.subzero.com
P: 800-222-7820

U-LINE
(BUILT-IN APPLIANCES)
www.u-line.com
P: 414-354-0300

VENTAHOOD
(HOODS)
www.ventahood.com
P: 972-235-5201

VIKING
(BUILT-IN APPLIANCES)
www.vikingrange.com
P: 888-845-4641

WM. OHS
(CABINETRY)
www.wmohs.com
P: 303-371-6550

WOODMODE
(CABINETRY)
www.wood-mode.com

FURNITURE AND ACCESSORIES

ALESSI
(ACCESSORIES)
www.alessi.com
P: 877-253-7749

BARNEYS
(ACCESSORIES AND LINENS)
P: 888-8-BARNEY

BERGDORF GOODMAN
(ACCESSORIES)
P: 800-558-1855

BRIDGE KITCHENWARE
(ACCESSORIES)
www.bridgekitchenware.com
P: 212-688-4220

BROADWAY PAN-HANDLER
(ACCESSORIES)
www.broadwaypanhandler.com
P: 866-COOKWARE

CHEF'S CATALOG
(ACCESSORIES)
www.chefscatalog.com
P: 800-884-CHEF

COOKING.COM
(ACCESSORIES)
www.cooking.com
P: 800-663-8810

CUISINART
(ACCESSORIES)
www.cuisinart.com
P: 800-726-0190

DEAN & DELUCA
(FINE FOODS, GIFTS)
www.deandeluca.com
P: 877-826-9246

GUMPS
(ACCESSORIES)
www.gumps.com
P: 800-436-4311

IKEA
(FURNITURE AND ACCESSORIES)
www.ikea-usa.com

KITCHENAID
(ACCESSORIES)
www.kitchenaid.com
P: 800-541-6390

KRUPS
(ACCESSORIES)
www.krups.com
P: 800-526-5377

MOLTENI
(CONTEMPORARY ITALIAN FURNITURE)
www.molteni.it
P: 201-585-9420

OXO
(ACCESSORIES)
www.oxo.com
P: 800-545-4111

POTTERY BARN
(ACCESSORIES)
www.potterybarn.com
P: 888-779-5176

RENOVATOR'S SUPPLY
(ACCESSORIES)
www.rensup.com
P: 800-659-2211

RÖSLE
(ACCESSORIES)
www.rosleusa.com
P: 302-326-4801

STELTON
(ACCESSORIES)
www.stelton.com
P: 651-690-0060

SUR LA TABLE
(ACCESSORIES)
www.surlatable.com
P: 800-243-0852 (ordering)
P: 866-328-5412
(customer service)

TARGET
(ACCESSORIES)
www.target.com
P: 800-440-0680

THE CONRAN SHOP
(FURNITURE AND
ACCESSORIES)
www.conran.com
P: 866-755-9079

WILLIAMS-SONOMA
(FURNITURE AND
ACCESSORIES)
www.williams-sonoma.com
P: 877-812-6235

TILES

AMTICO
(STONE, GLASS, MOSAICS,
CERAMIC, MARBLE,
GRANITE, SHELL)
www.amtico.com
P: 800-268-4260

ANN SACKS
(STONE, GLASS, MOSAICS,
CERAMIC, PORCELAIN)
www.annsacks.com
P: 800-278-8453

ARTISTIC TILE
(STONE, GLASS, MOSAICS,
CERAMIC, PORCELAIN)
www.artistictile.com
P: 800-260-8646

BISAZZA
(GLASS MOSAICS)
www.bisazzausa.com

COUNTRY FLOORS
(STONE, TERRA COTTA,
MOSAICS)
www.countryfloors.com
P: 800-311-9995

DUPONT
(TILING)
www.corian.com
P: 800-4-CORIAN

EMAUX DE BRIARE
(TILING)
www.emauxdebriare.com
P: 516-931-6924

HASTINGS TILE
(STONE, MOSAICS,
GLASS, PORCELAIN)
www.hastingstilebath.com
P: 516-379-3500

PARIS CERAMICS
(CERAMIC)
www.parisceramics.com
P: 888-845-3487

WALKER ZANGER
(STONE, CERAMIC)
www.walkerzanger.com
P: 877-611-0199

WE WOULD LIKE TO THANK THE OWNERS, DECORATORS, INSTITUTIONS OR HOTELS THAT HAVE WELCOMED *ELLE DECOR* **COLLABORATORS FOR THEIR REPORTAGES:**
PIERRE ARDITI, LINDA ARSCHOOT AND HER HUSBAND SWEET LOVE, CHRISTIAN ASTUGUEVIEILLE, DOMINIQUE BABIGEON, VANNA BELLAZZI, CHRISTIAN BENAIS, PIERRE BERGE, GREGOIRE BIGNIER, JACQUES BON (HÔTEL DU MAS DE PEINT), GUY BRETON, FRANÇOIS CATROUX, AGNES COMAR, DAVID CHAMPION, ANTHONY COLLETT, AGNÈS COMAR, TERENCE CONRAN, DANI (D. ROSE), ALAIN DEMACHY, RENA DUMAS, CHRISTIAN DUVAL, MONIQUE DUVEAU, LOULOU DE LA FALAISE, MAXIME DE LA FALAISE, B. AND O. FOURET, ANNICK GOUTAL, FRANÇOIS-JOSEPH GRAF, JACQUES GRANGE, CHRISTINE AND MICHEL GUERARD, MARC HELD, PATRICIA AND PHILIPPE HUREL, MICHELE JOUBERT, DONNA KARAN, CALVIN KLEIN, NICOLE LEHMANN, BRUNO LE MOULT, JOHN MAC LEOD, GENEVIEVE LETHU, CHRISTIAN LIAIGRE, MARIE-JO MAZE-CENSIER, FREDERIC MECHICHE, JEAN-LOUIS AND MADO MELLERIO, JEAN ODDES, JEAN-LAURENT PERIER, ERIC POISSON, ANDREE PUTMAN, ALAIN RAYNAUD, ESTELLE REALE-GARCIN, BERNARD ROUX, SARAH SAINT-GEORGE, VALERIE SOLVIT, PHILIPPE STARCK, REMI TESSIER, ROGER SOUVEYRENS AND WALDA PAIRON, SUSIE TOMPKINS-BUELL, KEES VAN DER VALK, AXEL VERHOUSTRAETEN, EDOUARD VERMEULEN, HERVE VERMESCH, ANDREW AND JILL ZARZYCKI.

Photo credits:

Guillaume de Laubier: pp. 10, 13, 18-19, 20, 22-23, 27 left, 31, 46-47, 51, 56-57, 62-63, 64, 67, 70-71, 74 to 77, 82, 83, 86 right, 89, 92, 93, 95, 121.
Marianne Haas: pp. 8, 12 top, 21, 25, 26, 27 right, 32, 36, 40, 41, 43, 48, 59, 61, 65, 66, 69, 88.
Jacques Dirand: pp. 16, 17, 24, 28-29, 30, 39, 44, 50, 53, 54, 72, 80-81, 86 left, 119.
Olivier Léger: pp. 110 to 117 (1, 2, 3, 5, 6, 9 to 15, 17, 18, 21, 23, 24, 26, 27, 28, 30 to 32 to 37, 39 to 45).
Gilles de Chabaneix: pp. 14, 15, 33, 34, 35, 38, 49, 55, 73, 78.
Patrice Pascal: pp. 94, 96-97, 98 to 101, 104 to 109, 118.
Guy Pascal: pp. 110 to 117 (4, 7, 8, 16, 19, 20, 22, 25, 29, 38).
Alain Gelberger: pp. 84-85, 87, 90, 91, 102, 103.
Alexandre Bailhache: pp. 12 bottom, 37, 68.
Gilles Bensimon: p. 9.
Edouard Sicot: p. 42.
Patrick Smith: p. 45.
Joël Laiter: p. 52.
Jérôme Darblay: p. 60.
Daniel Boudinet: p. 78.
François Halard: p. 120.

Reportages and production:

Marie-Claire Blanckaert: pp. 8, 10, 12 top, 13 to 15, 18-19, 20, 22-23, 25 to 27, 31, 32, 33, 36, 39, 42, 43, 45, 46-47, 50, 51, 56-57, 58, 59, 60, 62 to 65, 67, 70 à 77, 80 to 83, 86, 88, 89, 92, 93, 95, 121.
Catherine Scotto: pp. 84-85, 87, 90, 91, 102, 103, 110-117 (1, 2, 3, 5, 6, 9 to 15, 17, 18, 21, 23, 24, 26, 27, 28, 30 to 32 to 37, 39 to 45).
Marie-Claude Dumoulin: pp. 35, 49, 78 (with Françoise Ayxendri), 110 to 117 (4, 7, 8, 16, 19, 20, 22, 25, 29, 38).
Barbara Bourgois: pp. 40, 41, 96-97, 98, 99, 104 to 109, 118.
Françoise Labro: pp. 21, 28-29, 30, 44, 48, 61.
François Baudot: pp. 9, 12 bottom, 16, 120.
Misha de Potestad: pp. 94, 100, 101.
Alexandra d'Arnoux: pp. 37, 78.
Marie Kalt: pp. 17, 34, 54, 119.
Elsa Simon: pp. 24, 53.
Fabienne Genevard: p. 38.
Olivia Phélip and Monique Duveau: p. 52.
Catherine de Chabaneix: p. 55.
Paul-Marie Sorel: p. 68.
Milu Cachat: p. 69.
D.M. Mourier: p. 66.

Elle Decor (U.S.) and *Elle Decoration* (France) are both imprints of the Hachette Filipacchi group.
The content of these books was taken solely from *Elle Decoration* and appeared only in France.

**Under the direction of
Jean Demachy**

Editorial
Marie-Claire Blanckaert

Art Direction
Anne-Marie Chéret

Editing
Claire Cornubert

Photo research
Sandrine Hess